PHOTOBOOTH
—DOGS—

PHOTOBOOTH
—DOGS—

CAMERON WOO

CHRONICLE BOOKS
SAN FRANCISCO

Library of Congress Cataloging-in-Publication Data available.
ISBN 978-0-8118-7251-5

Manufactured in China.

Designed by Supriya Kalidas.
For photograph credits, see pages 106–107.

10 9 8 7 6 5 4 3 2 1

Chronicle Books LLC
680 Second Street
San Francisco, California 94107
www.chroniclebooks.com

{ TO **NELLIE**, OUR SWEET GIRL }

INTRODUCTION

The "Photomaton," invented by Anatol Josepho and introduced to the public in 1927, has always been a place where, thanks to a curtain and a mechanical (unmanned) lens, you are free to be whomever you like. You can invent yourself or define yourself, unconstrained by decorum or expectation. You can be a vixen or a dog owner or a cowboy, or a vixenish cowboy dog owner: Once you have drawn that liberating curtain, the choice is yours alone.

When I look at these photos, it is lovely—and entertaining—to imagine the dogs (having heard about the photobooth) making their way to the bus station or the fairground to experience it for themselves. I picture them clambering onto the stool and waiting, just like everyone else, for the light to flash and the picture to emerge. It doesn't seem entirely out of the question; there really is something uncanny about the way dogs in photographs always look as though they're posing. If they stare at the camera, they look saucy; if they glance away, they appear coy. But either way, they look deliberate, which is at the very heart of the photobooth experience.

When you think about it, it just makes sense that dogs should make their appearance in photobooth pictures, either alone or with a partner. The photobooth is about document and about identity. It's a place to record, usually with an eye to the future, the things that are important to you—a fancy hat, a new beau, or, in the case of these images,

ANATOL JOSEPHO
Self-portrait of Anatol Josepho with terrier, 1928–30
International Center of Photography,
Gift of the Josepho family, 2008

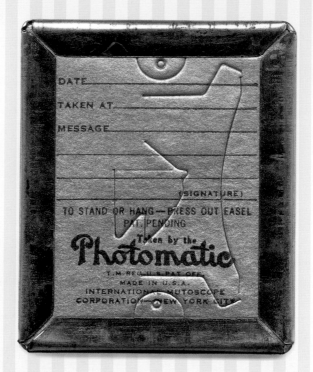

a best friend. It doesn't surprise me, then, to discover the photo-booth portrait of a dapper Anatol Josepho and his dog, dating back to 1928, a few short months after the Photomaton's introduction. I can imagine other early attempts to photograph man's best friend, thwarted by the attendants who, in the beginning, assisted those people who were unfamiliar with the booth. These combinations are as inevitable as any other portrait of a relationship, and often more long lasting.

What I love about these images, besides the small, brave dogs perched alone and somewhat precariously on rickety stools, is that the owners are as distinctive as their pets. And though over eighty years have passed since the photobooth first appeared on the scene, the pictures feel very contemporary. That is, if you love your dog enough to take him to a photobooth, you are bound to share certain characteristics with those of similar inclination—these images forge a link across time and space, from those long-gone dogs to the furry pal who sits by your side today.

BABBETTE HINES *author of* Photobooth *and "found" photograph collector*

{ A GOOD SNAPSHOT STOPS A MOMENT
FROM RUNNING AWAY. }

Eudora Welty

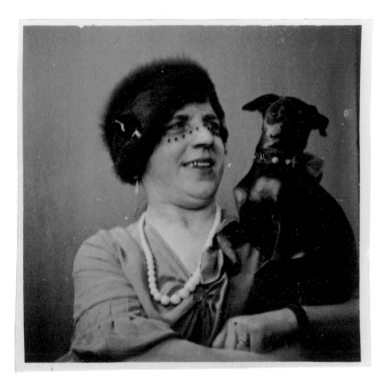

{ NO HOME IS COMPLETE WHICH DOES NOT INCLUDE
A DOG AS AN IMPORTANT MEMBER OF THE FAMILY. }

Robert Leighton
The Complete Book of the Dog

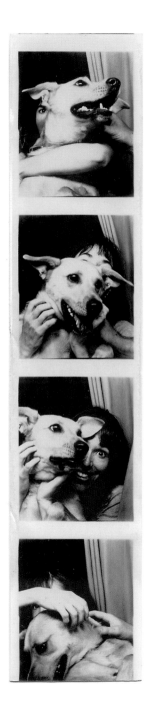

CREDITS

Courtesy of Barbara
Puorro Galasso

Courtesy of Gail Pine

Courtesy of
Babbette Hines

Courtesy of Barbara
Puorro Galasso

Courtesy of Barbara
Puorro Galasso

Courtesy of
Babbette Hines

Courtesy of
Pam Hastings
PAM WITH BUFFY
1963

Courtesy of John Berg
JOHN, JASPER, STEVE
1980

Courtesy of
Rayne Wolfe
MOM AND DUSTY
1940s

Courtesy of
Rayne Wolfe
MOM AND DUSTY
1940s

Courtesy of Lisa
and Lordan Bunch

Courtesy of Lisa
and Lordan Bunch

Courtesy of
Lisa Ann Kelly
JULIA AND SHEP *1930s*

Courtesy of
Tamera Herrod
WORLD'S FAIR *1939*

Courtesy of
Kara Keltner
MARU AND KARA
1980

Courtesy of Francisco "Rocky" Garcia
**DOLORES MENDEVIL, CHAMP, ROCKY GARCIA,
AND CARLOS RUBEN MILAN** *1960*

Courtesy of
Beth Burstein

Courtesy of John
and Teenuh Foster,
Accidental Mysteries
Collection

Courtesy of
Kimberly Hebert

Courtesy of
Greg McLemore

ACKNOWLEDGMENTS

I would like to thank the following for their invaluable assistance: Babbette Hines, the family of Anatol Josepho, and Ruth Silverman, plus Ursula Cary, Supriya Kalidas, and Kate Woodrow of Chronicle Books. A special note of appreciation is also due to all of the readers of our magazine, *The Bark*, who responded to our call for photobooth dog pictures with great generosity and enthusiasm.